WALKING WITH
GALATIANS

BECOME THE MAN GOD INTENDS YOU TO BE

Carriage
House
PUBLISHERS

A 30-DAY DEVOTIONAL
AND BIBLE STUDY

FRED J. PARRY

WALKING WITH GALATIANS

Published by
Carriage House Publishers

Library of Congress Control Number: (Application Pending)
Paperback ISBN: 979-8-9857824-8-6
eBook ISBN: 979-8-9857824-9-3
Cover Design by Debbie Lewis (Illumify Media)
Interior Design: Carolyn Preul
Editor: Sandy Selby
Theological Review: Gary Powell
Printed in the United States of America

ACKNOWLEDGMENT:

Special thanks to my friend, Pastor Gary Powell, for his expert guidance and theological review of *Walking With Galatians*.

Gary Powell is the founding pastor at The Revolution Church in Columbia, Missouri. He ministers to those who need healing and equips the believer through simple faith and belief in the Word to effectively do the same. He is married to Audra, and they have three kids. You can learn more about The Revolution at RevolutionColumbia.com.

This book is dedicated to the two women who had the greatest influence on my walk with Jesus, both of whom passed away while I was researching and writing this devotional.

Melody Garnett Parry, my incredible, Jesus-loving wife of 30 years, who died on May 23, 2023, at the age of 59 after a very short illness.

Nora Kathleen Holmes Parry, my accomplished and strong-willed mother who passed away on February 1, 2024, after an amazing 91 years on this planet.

I owe so much to these women. God blessed me in immeasurable ways by bringing these two unique women into my life. The assurance of God's promise of eternal life and the anticipation of our joyous reunion is what has sustained me through the loss.

I miss and love you both.

———————

Because of the Lord's great love we are not consumed,
for his compassions never fail.
They are new every morning;
great is your faithfulness.
I say to myself, "The Lord is my portion;
therefore, I will wait for him."

Lamentations 3:22-24 NIV

CONTENTS

For more information on using this book for a group study,
please visit **www.FredParry.Life** to access study materials,
handouts, and other useful information.

INTRODUCTION

SAVED BY GRACE

We are living in challenging times. It's hard to imagine a time when it was more difficult to live out what it means to be a man than it is today. Our traditional roles as providers and protectors are no longer sufficient for this ever-changing world, and there's a troubling lack of clarity on whether modern-day cultural standards will even allow us to provide and protect as was once the norm.

At the same time, we've found ourselves in the middle of an identity crisis of epic proportions where the male species is confused, distracted, and marginalized. We live in a world where men who have found themselves in positions of authority are simply ashamed to be men. They've surrendered to the wrong authority, who has accused them of "toxic masculinity" for simply attempting to do the right thing. Many have forfeited their "man cards" and have retreated to isolation. As you will read in the coming pages, that's a dangerous place for men to be.

Amid this confusion, there's never been a more important time to lean into God's truth. As you prepare to dive into Paul's letter to the Galatians, you'll discover that the ideals and principles he presented to Christians in Galatia are as relevant today as they were more than 2,000 years ago. While the challenges are different, the solutions are the same. Concepts like integrity, generosity, kindness, and grace never go out of style.

You'll discover in Paul's letter that he has become frustrated with false teachers in Galatia, who have been spreading misinformation about the gospel. Paul encourages these new Christians to check the motivations of those questioning God's promises to man. In this era, where all you need is a cell phone camera and a Tik Tok account to become an "influencer," the thin line between those you can trust and those you can't has become almost invisible. There's never been a more critical time to scrutinize the messages that are overwhelming our inboxes and social media feeds. Of greater concern is the misinformation sent to our children and young adults who lack the benefit of discernment.

One other central theme in Paul's letter to Galatia deals with the tension that exists between Jews and Gentiles. Paul, a Jew himself, expresses his displeasure that many Jews consider the Gentiles to be an unclean race, unworthy of equal standing before God. Things aren't much different today when you consider the levels of racism and prejudice throughout the world and the centuries-old conflict that still exists in the Middle East. As you contemplate our seeming lack of progress in these areas, it's important to remember that these are man-made problems and not the work of God. God has been consistent and steadfast in his insistence that we love and serve ALL our neighbors.

A central point of conflict in Galatians centers around the question of justification. By the end of the letter, it's clear that the death of Jesus on the cross was an acceptable sacrifice to make man right in the eyes of God. The death of Jesus paid the debt for man's sins and gave us a new freedom, ending our slavery under the law so that we could start doing good to honor God. Because of Jesus's selflessness, sinners are reborn and are now heirs to the throne. The gift of the Holy Spirit now lives in men so that we can start anew, living lives that please God.

There are so many valuable lessons that come from this important letter. You've heard the adage, "the more things change, the more they stay the same." So much of the wisdom in Paul's letter applies to our current times. Paul reminds us that we all have blind spots and that we need the counsel of trusted friends who will speak truth into our lives. And, speaking of friends, we are reminded, again, of our obligation to look out for one another and when one of us stumbles in life, it's our duty to help restore him and put him back on his feet.

While writing this devotional, one of Paul's messages resonated with me in a profound way. Paul speaks to the mystery surrounding God's timing. As men, we become frustrated when God doesn't immediately respond to our prayer requests even when the stakes are high. There's an uncanny wisdom in God's timing, and we must live with the confidence that his time and plan are good and perfect.

As you may have read in the dedication of this book, I lost my wife and mother in a matter of months while researching and writing this book. In complete transparency, I found great comfort in the timing of my mother's passing. She was 91 years old, suffered from dementia, and she was ready to be with Jesus. On the contrary, my wife, Melody, was only 59 years old when she passed after a short illness. She had courageously beaten cancer twice but succumbed to a rare and sudden lung disease, leaving me and my two sons in a deep state of loss and grief. While I don't understand the timing, I am completely confident that her passing was part of a good and perfect plan set in motion long before my wife was born. If not for my faith and the compassionate support of my band of Christian brothers, the losses I experienced in such a short time span would have defeated me.

Thanks to the wisdom gained from Paul's letter to the Galatians, I know I will survive this current trial. I don't like what happened to my wife, but I do trust God. There will be a time when God's plan in all of this will be revealed.

Finally, Paul's letter reminds his readers that because we have been saved by God's grace and his grace alone, we have a newfound freedom in our lives. With this freedom, we can either choose to continue to pursue sin or we can choose to pursue righteousness by serving one another. It's a conscious decision for each of us to make. One path leads to destruction. The other leads to living a life that pleases God.

I hope you find this study to be fulfilling and empowering.

I pray that you will allow God's word to transform your heart and renew your mind.

Fred J. Parry

MY PRAYER

God, thank you for the wisdom and encouragement shared by the Apostle Paul in Galatians. May you be revealed to us in the way Jesus revealed himself to Paul on the road to Damascus. Let your words and Paul's words resonate with us as they did thousands of years ago. Guide us as we continue to pursue you through the acts of love and service we extend to others. For these things, we pray in the name of your son, Jesus. Amen.

HOW TO USE THIS BOOK

Walking with Galatians is designed to serve the dual purpose of being a daily devotional and a Bible study guide for Paul's Epistle to the Galatians. While the book is structured to be used over a six-week period, I would encourage you to use it at a pace that is most comfortable for you.

Each of the daily devotions is inspired by one of Paul's messages in this important letter that reminds his readers of the significance of Christ's sacrificial death on the cross. From these messages, I have found themes that can guide us in our daily walk to become better Christians. These devotionals were written as responses from my own understanding of how a particular verse spoke to me. The goal of any Bible study is to find the correct interpretation, which leads to a variety of applications. That, in itself, is rightly handling the word of truth (2 Timothy 2:15).

If you're like me, you'll get a new insight or meaning each time you read one of these passages, and not because the Bible's meaning has changed, but because we, as individuals, have changed since the last time we were there. We've become more aware of a different aspect of our lives, and this scripture now speaks to us in a new way. We are more teachable than we were before. The Bible takes us on where we are, and God uses His

Word to lead us to greater maturity and a broader perspective. The Bible is as deep as we are and deeper still.

I would suggest approaching each devotional in prayer, asking God for clarity of mind and focus with a hope that the day's message resonates with you in some meaningful way.

Once you've read the devotional, you'll find the following tools at the end of each reading to help you get the most meaning out of the day's message:

- a reference to scripture outside Galatians that will reinforce and add context to the day's message.
- two short questions designed to help you apply that day's lesson to your life.
- a call to contemplation, which is intended as a prompt for journaling. It's an excellent opportunity to explore and record your feelings as they relate to the day's message.

To gain a better understanding of the literary and cultural context of each day's passage, I would encourage you to refer to the full text each day to fully understand the contextual circumstances and events surrounding each passage.

I hope that you will find these devotionals to be useful and relevant in your daily walk. My prayer is that the wisdom that comes from Paul's letter to the Galatians will guide you in your journey to lead a more fulfilling and Christ-centered life.

FJP

BACKGROUND

THE APOSTLE PAUL

Paul was born in the city of Tarsus, a major city in eastern Cilicia on the trade route between Syria and Asia Minor, located in the same geographical region as modern-day Turkey. Born the son of a Pharisee and in the ancestral lineage of the Tribe of Benjamin, Paul enjoyed the unique distinction of being a Jew and the privilege of being a Roman citizen. He could speak Hebrew, but his native tongue was Koine Greek. Paul was educated at the prestigious Rabbinical school taught by the Rabbi Gamaliel, who was one of the most influential rabbis of ancient Judaism.

Paul is among the most important figures in the history and growth of Christianity. He is the author of 13 of the 27 books in the New Testament. While there is some scholarly debate as to the complete authenticity of some of the books in the New Testament, experts acknowledge that at least seven of the 13 books from Paul are undisputed as authentic works.

PAUL'S CONVERSION

Readers of the New Testament first encounter Paul as "Saul of Tarsus." Though Saul was a tentmaker by trade, he was a fervent persecutor of early Christians. In Acts 9:1-22, we read of Saul traveling from Jerusalem to Damascus during his crusade to arrest disciples when he encounters the resurrected Jesus in a great light. During this experience, Jesus reveals to Saul that he is Lord and that persecuting his followers is the same as persecuting the Lord Jesus and is, in effect, fighting against God. N.T. Wright conjectures that during this journey, Paul was repeating a prayer, used by many serious Jews in his day, requesting a visionary experience of God. An answer to that prayer was surprising enough but seeing Jesus in the place of Yahweh literally reconfigured Paul's worldview.

During this encounter, Saul was temporarily blinded by the light that surrounded the vision of Jesus. Despite this, he traveled on to Damascus where he remained blind for three days. Saul took

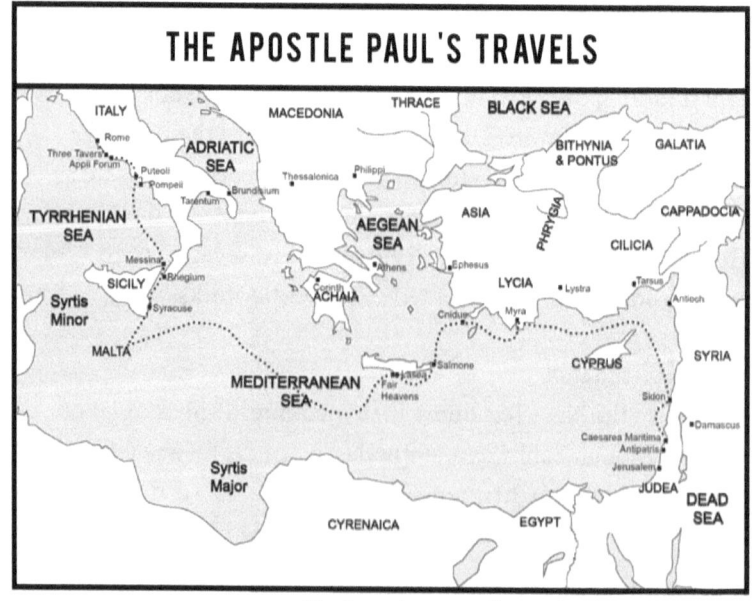

Map Copyright 2021 • Walking With Galatians • Fred J. Parry

no food or water for this period and stayed in a constant state of prayer until approached by a disciple named Ananias. Ananias told Saul that Jesus had sent him to restore his sight and assured Saul that the Lord would fill him with the Holy Spirit. Once Saul's sight was restored, he was immediately baptized and became a fervent believer in Jesus Christ.

PAUL'S MISSIONARY TRIPS

Following his baptism, Paul went on to Arabia and Damascus and began to preach that Jesus was the Messiah. It was soon thereafter that he, himself, began to be persecuted for his teachings. Around A.D. 37, nearly three years after his conversion, Paul traveled to Jerusalem where he met for 15 days with James, the half-brother of Jesus, and the apostle Peter. Paul used these meetings to learn more about the life of Jesus and to report on his efforts in preaching about the Kingdom of God and Jesus the Messiah. Over time, Paul became known as the "Apostle to the Gentiles," while Peter would assume the role "Apostle to the Jews."

Soon after Paul met with James and Peter, he returned to his hometown of Tarsus to preach until Barnabas invited him to go and teach at the rapidly growing church in Antioch. It was there where Paul began to build a network of house churches, where the earliest Christians would gather at the homes of other followers until the size of the group forced them to divide into smaller groups. Antioch was also the first place where Jewish-Gentile churches took root.

With limited resources, Paul and Barnabas often relied on the generosity of their converts for food and housing. In A.D. 47,

Paul returned to Jerusalem with Barnabas and brought famine relief contributed by the early churches they had started. In doing so, Paul honored the request made by Peter and James and, was, perhaps, the earliest pioneer of missionary work that would be done by churches throughout the coming centuries.

In Acts 15, Paul and Barnabas participated in the Council of Jerusalem (circa AD 48–50), where they met with James, Peter, and John to discuss whether Gentile converts needed to be circumcised and conform with Mosaic law and other strict Jewish rituals to be considered legitimate Christians. It was at this gathering where it was determined that circumcision would not be a requirement for Gentile converts to become part of God's new covenant.

Paul and Barnabas, soon thereafter, set out from Antioch on the first of three mission trips where they visited Cyprus and Galatia. It was around this time that Saul began to be more commonly referred to as Paul. Historians speculate that Paul was Saul's Roman name and that the names may have been used interchangeably so that he could more easily relate to diverse audiences.

After parting ways with Barnabas in Antioch, Paul chose Silas (Silvanus) to accompany him to Syria and Cilicia to reinforce Paul's work with the churches he had previously established there. Their travels led them to Derbe and to Lystra, where they met Timothy, who was well-respected in the area. He was the son of a Jewish woman and a Greek father. As the three traveled through Phrygia and Galatia, Paul had a vision one night of a man from

Macedonia pleading for them to come to that region. The next morning, they departed immediately, sailing from Troas on a course to Samothrace, Neapolis, and then to Philippi.

When Paul exorcised the demons from a slave girl, he and Silas were imprisoned in Philippi for a short time. Once released from captivity, they left Philippi. From there they traveled through Amphipolis and Apollonia before arriving in Thessalonica.

FROM ASIA TO EUROPE

Thessalonica was the home of an important dockyard situated on the harbor of the Thermaic Gulf in the northwest corner of the Aegean Sea near the junction of the Egnatian Way and the road that led north to the Danube. Built by the Romans as their primary route east to Byzantium, the Egnatian Way was nearly 700 miles long at the time. The roadway was nearly 20 feet wide and paved with large stone slabs topped off by a hardened layer of sand. It traversed several mountain passes and river gorges providing travelers a direct connection between Rome and the Aegean Sea.

Thessalonica thrived because of its location along this major trade route to the east into Asia and west to Rome, becoming a city known for its prosperity and cultural activity. Located 100 miles southwest of Philippi, Thessalonica eventually became the capital of the Roman province of Macedon. Thessalonica was a thriving city of nearly 200,000 citizens in Macedonia in Northern Greece. The city still exists but is now known as Thessaloniki.

Paul's trip to Thessalonica was significant because it was the beginning of spreading the gospel from Asia to Europe.

Tragically, Paul's time in Thessalonica was cut short by mob-led persecution. He fled the region and traveled on to Berea, but angry mobs there forced him to move on again to Athens for a short time. Paul eventually settled in Corinth.

In 1 Corinthians 2:3, we learn that Paul had become fearful and very discouraged with the fruits of his missionary work. He deeply regretted leaving his new believers before they were established in their faith. The imprisonment, persecution, and treatment by angry mobs had taken a toll on Paul. He became concerned about the churches he had planted and worried about their viability.

THE CAPTIVITY EPISTLES

Throughout his ministry life, Paul was jailed on numerous occasions and placed under house arrest for extended periods. It was during these periods that Paul crafted several of his letters to the churches he had planted. Because these letters were written while he was imprisoned, they are often referred to as the "Captivity Epistles."

In Acts 16:16-34, while Paul was imprisoned in Philippi, a sudden earthquake brought down the walls of the jail. Paul and Silas made the conscious decision to not escape, and this would lead to a trusted relationship with their jailer, who became a follower of Christ. In A.D. 57, Paul returned to Jerusalem and was soon arrested and jailed for taking a Gentile too far into the precincts of the temple. These were false accusations, based on faulty assumptions, but they caused enough upheaval to gain the attention of Roman authorities (Acts 22:29).

During his captivity in Jerusalem, Paul defended his actions before the Sanhedrin. His testimony divided the Sadducees and Pharisees, who had strong disagreements over whether Paul had broken any laws. Roman authorities then took Paul, with an armed escort, to Caesarea for higher officials to hear the case. Paul remained there for several years and despite his innocence, he was not released. Biblical tradition reports that a Roman official was trying to extort a bribe from him in exchange for his release, but Paul refused (Acts 24:26). Finally, exasperated, Paul asked to make an appeal to Caesar himself. After his request was reluctantly granted, Paul was placed on a ship as a prisoner to sail to Rome. On that voyage, he was shipwrecked on the island of Malta for three months where he performed miracles and continued to preach the word of God.

When Paul finally arrived in Rome, he was placed under house arrest but was allowed to continue preaching without interruption from authorities. During this time, Paul wrote his letters to the Philippians, Ephesians, Colossians, and Philemon. Upon his release, it is believed that Paul then traveled to Spain, where he wrote his letters to Timothy and Titus.

PAUL'S DEATH SENTENCE

In A.D. 64, Paul returned to Rome, where he was martyred. While little has been written regarding the details surrounding Paul's death, tradition has it that Paul was sentenced to death by Roman Emperor Nero. Paul's death sentence came shortly after a large portion of Rome, filled mostly with tenements for the poor, burned in a fire. Nero blamed the fire on Christians, though Roman documents suggest that Nero started the fire himself to clear the area for a building project. Because Paul was a Roman citizen, he was exempt from death by crucifixion. Instead, he was decapitated by a sword. In the end, Paul died because of his faith. In his final writings, it was clear that Paul was ready and willing to die for Christ. He gave his last breath for the cause of helping the first generation of Christians understand that sacrifice was an integral part of following Christ.

FJP

OVERVIEW OF PAUL'S EPISTLE TO GALATIANS

ABOUT GALATIA

Galatia was one of the provinces located in Asia Minor, the area now known as modern-day Turkey. It is not far from the city of Tarsus in the province of Cilicia, where the Apostle Paul was born. The Galatians were a Celtic people that migrated to the region in the third century from Gaul, the area now known as France. The Roman Empire conquered Galatia in 189 BC but afforded its citizens an extraordinary amount of autonomy before finally making it a Roman province in 25 BC. The Apostle Paul established churches in the southern Galatian cities of Pisidian Antioch, Iconium, Lystra, and Derbe during the first of his three missionary trips. The founding of each of these churches is referenced in the Book of Acts.

PAUL'S EPISTLE TO GALATIANS

Biblical scholars believe that Paul's letter to Galatians was written around AD 49 and is likely his earliest epistle. The letter was written during the reign of Roman Emperor Claudius and after Paul had attended the Jerusalem Council. Galatians is the only letter written by Paul that was addressed to churches in multiple cities.

The overriding purpose of Paul's letter to Galatians was to rebuke the false teachings of Judaizers who had infiltrated churches in Galatia. They were attempting to undermine Paul's teachings on justification and the details surrounding the life, death, and resurrection of Christ. Judaizers falsely claimed that simply having faith in Jesus Christ was not enough to be in good standing with God. These critics of Paul believed that his teachings had strayed too far from his Jewish roots, accusing him of trying to simply appease new converts by telling them what they wanted to hear.

The tone of Paul's letter to the Galatian churches makes no attempt to hide his disappointment and frustration. Of Paul's 13 letters included in the New Testament, Galatians is the only letter that does not begin with a traditional greeting or expression of thanksgiving to its intended recipients. Instead, Paul gets right to the point in describing his incredulity with those in the Galatian churches who had fallen victim to the false teachings, straying from the true gospel he had preached while establishing those churches.

While many of the themes referenced in Galatians are like those included in Paul's letter to the Roman church, Galatians provides a wealth of historical information about Paul not found in other sections of the Bible. This includes details about his three-year stay in Arabia and his 15-day visit in Jerusalem with Peter and James, the half-brother of Jesus. Galatians also provides the only account of Paul's stern rebuke of Peter in Antioch where Peter, allegedly under pressure from critics in Jerusalem, refused to take part in fellowship with a group of Gentile Christians. Other themes introduced in Galatians include the concept of justification and the redemptive-historical context of God's new creation.

Paul also hoped to make it abundantly clear that the law of Moses could not take precedent over the covenant which God had made with Abraham some 430 years earlier. The cross on which Jesus was crucified was the one and only way to salvation and the absolute proof of God honoring his covenant with Abraham. No amount of works, good deeds, human achievement, or even strict obedience to Mosaic law could trump the sacrifice made by Jesus on behalf of sinners ... past, present, and future. The death of Christ on the cross eliminated the need to adhere to Mosaic law because it delivered forgiveness of sin and made humankind righteous in the eyes of God.

THE APOSTLE TO THE GENTILES

Through a division of responsibilities, it was established that Peter (Cephas) would be the apostle to the Jews and Paul would be considered the apostle to the Gentiles. However, Paul was not the first to share the gospel of Jesus Christ with the Gentiles. In Acts 10, we find the story of Peter being sent by God to share the gospel with Cornelius, a Roman centurion. Paul's status as a true apostle, however, was called into question by Judaizers who claimed that Paul's understanding of Jesus Christ had come only through second-hand accounts passed on to him by some of the original apostles who knew and worked with Christ. Paul vigorously rebuked that claim, pointing to his encounter with the resurrected Jesus on the road to Damascus. He made it clear that he did not go and sit at the feet of Peter, James, and John to learn about Jesus. On the contrary, he instead got his information through the revelation of Jesus Christ himself.

Despite the claims made by his detractors, Paul had impeccable credentials as a Jew. As is recorded in Philippians 3:1-9, Paul was born a Hebrew, circumcised on the customary eighth day, and was of the lineage of the tribe of Benjamin. He was a Pharisee, educated by the Rabbi Gamaliel, and was a zealous persecutor of the early Christian church. Before becoming a follower of Christ, he considered himself to be righteous under Mosaic law.

MOVING FORWARD

Over the next 40 years, the prevalence of churches where Jews and Gentiles worshipped together would expand throughout the Roman Empire. Urban Gentile population centers would replace Israel as the epicenter of Christianity. The destruction of Jerusalem in AD 70 would shift the church's center to Antioch in Syria. The threat of Jewish legalism on Christianity eventually faded. Over time, the most disruptive threats to Christianity would not come from legalistic Jews, atheism, or even Pagan religions but rather from those within the Christian religion who would choose to refute scriptural and biblical truths in the hope of shaping church doctrine to meet their own needs and justify their sin-laden desires. The letters written by Paul to the various churches were indeed for everyone and would eventually become recognized as scripture inspired by the Holy Spirit.

FJP

They only heard the report:
"The man who formerly persecuted us is now
preaching the faith he once tried to destroy."

Galatians 1:23 NIV

WEEK 1

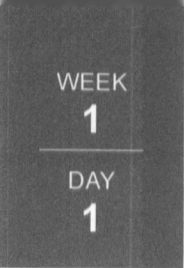
PEOPLE PLEASING

Am I now trying to win the approval of human beings, or of God? Or am I trying to please people? If I were still trying to please people, I would not be a servant of Christ. Galatians 1:10 NIV

Have you ever had to compromise your values for the sake of earning the approval of a new friend, a promotion at work, or just acceptance into a new group of friends? If you have, you're certainly not alone. Most of us have a deep desire to be connected and accepted by others. Unfortunately, "getting along" may require us to go along with something that seems wrong. We do not want to draw scrutiny or rejection from someone who might be our ticket to increased popularity or status among our peers. The Apostle Paul made it clear to the Galatians that he had no interest in winning a popularity contest and was relentless in rebuking the claims of the Judaizers.

Paul refused to find middle ground with those who were trying to discredit his teachings on how one might earn God's approval. His detractors claimed that Jewish Christians would be required to adhere to Mosaic law and ceremonial traditions that had been in place for centuries. One of those traditions required male believers to be circumcised. Paul insisted that it was by faith, and faith alone, that man could be made right with God. If one had accepted Christ Jesus by faith, nothing more was necessary to earn God's favor—not even strict adherence to the Ten Commandments. For Paul, this truth was nonnegotiable and not subject to any other interpretation.

Paul had great empathy for his new believers, but zero tolerance for the Judaizers who were putting forth false information. While it would have been easier for Paul to appease his critics by softening his stance, he was willing to wage a war over the truths he had learned from his revelation with Jesus on the road to Damascus.

The world is full of people wanting us to set aside our core values and principles for the sake of temporary pleasure or to satisfy their selfish needs. Unfortunately, too often, our strong desire for acceptance leads us down the path to making a series of bad choices. It is said that if we fail to stand for something, we are likely to fall for anything. Paul was not interested in pleasing man. His heart was set on pleasing God. His steadfast adherence to principle over popularity is a model for any man who desires to become the best version of himself. When it comes to integrity and character, there's no room for compromise in our lives.

MY PRAYER

Father God, give me the courage to stand firm in my decision to lead a life that pleases you rather than my fellow man. Protect my heart from the temptation to make the kind of choices that only provide temporary pleasure and give me a thirst to pursue the things that offer an eternal reward. I pray for these things in the name of your son, Jesus Christ. Amen.

READ: ROMANS 14:1-23

QUESTION #1: Under what circumstances are you most likely to compromise on your core values?

QUESTION #2: What steps can you take to maintain stronger convictions regarding your integrity and character?

CONTEMPLATE

Recall a time when you felt pressure to compromise on your personal values with another person. What was the outcome?

A TRANSFORMED LIFE

They only heard the report: "The man who formerly persecuted us is now preaching the faith he once tried to destroy..." Galatians 1:23 NIV

Have you ever witnessed another person completely turn their lives around? Maybe it was a friend who once struggled with addiction or a successful young man who had been in trouble with the law as a teenager. These turnaround stories can inspire us and others to believe in the power of second chances and one's own ability to change. Unfortunately, these kinds of transformations are more the exception than the rule. Our experiences with personal failure leave us with deep-seated skepticism over our ability to make wholesale changes in our lives.

The Galatians and Judaizers were having a tough time reconciling the fact that Paul, once a prolific persecutor of Christians, could now be one of Christianity's most passionate promoters. Not all of us will experience a catalytic event like the blinding revelation of Paul's encounter with Jesus, but it is indeed possible for a man's heart to be changed in dramatic ways. When we beat the odds of addiction or decide to surrender our lives to Christ, those who know us best will recognize the transformation. They will see the changes in our lives and celebrate our successes. More importantly, others will be inspired to initiate this kind of change in their own lives. They will also be curious about the reason for the hope that comes with a transformed life.

If we can commit ourselves to consistency and doggedly building upon our initial success, others will take note and feel a greater sense of confidence regarding the possibility of changing their lives. True transformation never comes easy or without sacrifice. Creating lasting change requires diligence and a laser-like focus on the rewards and benefits that come from living a transformed life. Because Paul was disciplined and uncompromising in his journey, others found his claims to be credible. The same can work for us.

What part of your life would benefit from transformation? Are you willing to do the work it requires? Our best path to success is to access God's empowering grace and admit that we are powerless to do this on our own. Without God, we can do nothing, but with God, nothing is impossible. The good news is that God is eagerly anticipating your decision to commit to change. You are a caterpillar that can become a beautiful butterfly; God has already laid the groundwork for your metamorphic moment. Embrace this invitation, and let the transformation begin.

MY PRAYER

God, help me to recognize the parts of my life where change is needed. Give me the wisdom to acknowledge my weakness and then the confidence to take action. Surround me with people who will encourage me and cheer me on to the victory you already have planned for me. I pray for these things in the name of your son, Jesus. Amen.

READ: EPHESIANS 4:20-24

QUESTION #1: What part of your life would benefit from some form of transformation?

QUESTION #2: How might you help and support others who are trying to change their lives?

CONTEMPLATE

What are the steps you can begin taking to become the best version of yourself? What are the lessons that can be learned from Paul's transformation?

REMEMBERING THE POOR

All they asked was that we should continue to remember the poor, the very thing I had been eager to do all along. Galatians 2:10 NIV

Because Paul was not one of the original 12 apostles who spent time with Jesus, his credibility was often called into question by his detractors. After his encounter with Jesus, Paul spent several years in the desert studying scripture before traveling to meet with original apostles Peter and John, and with James, the half-brother of Jesus. Paul used these opportunities to confirm that his teaching was indeed consistent with the teaching of those who were closest to Jesus. While sending him on his way to continue his ministry to non-Jews, Peter and John encouraged Paul to pay special attention to caring for the poor. The church in Jerusalem was experiencing a significant famine at the time and the apostles urged Paul to emphasize Jesus's compassion and Christians' obligation to take care of those in need.

More than 2,000 years after Paul's humanitarian efforts to help the poor, the ravages of poverty and hunger are still prevalent in much of the world. Peter and John's message about helping the poor among us is as relevant today as it was then. Today, more than 10 percent of the world is living below the international poverty line. That's more than 800 million people. Poverty and hunger are no longer relegated to third world countries. Due to poor economic conditions and a lack of opportunity in so many cities, people in our very own communities are now experiencing staggering levels of food insecurity and impoverished living conditions. The problem is real, and it exists right here in our own backyards. As Christians, we are called to own it. This calling extends beyond a simple financial transaction. We should challenge ourselves to develop a lifestyle of generosity, which includes giving freely of our time, love, and counsel.

In Matthew 25:35-40, Jesus reminds us that whatever we do for the least of our brothers, we are essentially doing that same thing for him. There is no ambiguity in his call to feed the hungry, take care of the sick, and provide shelter for strangers; it is a direct message regarding our obligations to people in need. The best way to show our love for God is to love and serve our neighbors.

As men, we often become consumed by our desire to meet our own needs first. Unfortunately, there's not much left for others after that happens. If we could become intentional about giving the first fruits of the harvest to God and to those in need, there's no doubt that our love and generosity will be rewarded in immeasurable ways.

MY PRAYER

Father, God, give me the heart to walk in the shoes of those less fortunate. Instill in me a sense of knowing that the first fruits of my work should be for the benefit of others and not for myself. Make me ever mindful that the things I do for the least of my brothers I am doing for you, my loving father. I pray for these things in the name of your son, Jesus. Amen.

READ: MATTHEW 25:35-40

QUESTION #1: In what ways could you be more intentional in your efforts to take care of the poor?

QUESTION #2: What are the opportunities that exist in your community to help the poor?

CONTEMPLATE

Write about the hesitation you feel regarding giving to the poor before taking care of your own needs.

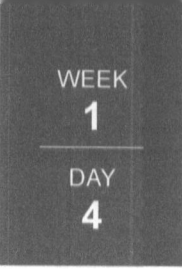

LIVING CONSISTENTLY

For before certain men came from James, he used to eat with the Gentiles. But when they arrived, he began to draw back and separate himself from the Gentiles because he was afraid of those who belonged to the circumcision group. Galatians 2:12 NIV

In this passage from Galatians, we learn about Paul's dissatisfaction with Peter's hypocrisy while in the presence of Jewish guests who refused to eat at the same table with Gentiles. Though Peter normally ate with Gentiles, he was hesitant to do so when these guests were present. Peter knew these Jews would disapprove of the "unclean" company he was keeping. Like many men, Peter was living a sort of compartmentalized life, and Paul strongly objected to his inconsistent behavior. Today, many of us live double lives. We operate by one set of values at church on Sunday morning and by another set at happy hour on Friday evening. Going with the flow and adjusting our behavior to match the moment can be a slippery slope.

If you wanted to hang with the cool kids in high school, you knew better than to be seen associating with a nerdy kid, even if he was your next door neighbor and a lifelong friend. We've come a long way since high school, but there's still a tendency for us to lead double lives. The challenge of trying to manage more than one lifestyle can be overwhelming. Our actions are often driven by the fear of what others may think about us, so rather than being able to be ourselves, we place a greater importance on how others view us. This can lead to destructive and sinful behavior.

The key to consistent living begins with becoming the kind of person you can love and be comfortable with. Once you shed the need to be accepted by anyone other than God, you can begin the process of becoming a person others will admire and respect. The simple exercise of embracing a set of core values and then adhering to them in any situation can make a dramatic difference. Imagine the kind of life you could lead if you placed your highest priority on personal values such as integrity, compassion, empathy, and honoring God. If these characteristics became your focus and you lived by these guideposts everyday, there's no doubt that you would become a better man.

MY PRAYER

God, I pray that I can learn to live a life that honors you with no concern for how others may view me. Give me the perseverance to live consistently and by a set of values that leads me to my full potential as a human being. I pray for these things in the name of your son, Jesus. Amen.

READ: 2 CORINTHIANS 10:12

QUESTION #1: What are the different compartments in your existing life where your behavior may vary from one situation to the next?

QUESTION #2: Name three core values you would like to embrace and make a priority in your life.

CONTEMPLATE

Write a mission statement for your life based on the core values you have decided to adopt. What are the steps you can take to begin living by this new vision?

TOUGH CONVERSATIONS

When I saw that they were not acting in line with the truth of the gospel, I said to Cephas in front of them all, "You are a Jew, yet you live like a Gentile and not like a Jew. How is it, then, that you force Gentiles to follow Jewish customs?" Galatians 2:14 NIV

While it might be contrary to the image people hold of the stereotypical, modern-day male, most men are somewhat passive in the face of conflict. We do not like confrontation, especially when we are being called out by another male for our indiscretions or weaknesses. I am sure there's a deeply psychological explanation for this behavior, but the truth is we would rather keep moving through our day without interruption or drama. Paul's irritation with Cephas (Peter) in this moment was obvious, and Paul's deep convictions about Peter's hypocrisy led him to directly confront Peter. Paul was bold. He did not choose to call Peter a hypocrite behind his back; he challenged Peter to his face.

There are times when we could all benefit from an uncomfortably tough conversation. Every one of us occasionally needs to have someone speak truth into our lives, and we should position ourselves to receive that truth. Unfortunately, so many of us have built fortified walls around our emotions and rarely give anyone permission to get that close. We march through life unable to see our own blind spots. Living without a clear understanding of our idiosyncrasies, bad habits, and dangerous liaisons puts us at a clear disadvantage. Even though Paul was calling Peter out in public, he was doing him a favor. He knew that Peter's inconsistent behavior would cost him credibility among the people who needed him most.

Perhaps you've heard the expression, "Every man needs a Paul, a Timothy, and a Barnabas." Timothy represents a man for whom we can mentor.

Barnabas is the guy who will encourage us through life's greatest storms. Paul is the man who speaks truth into our lives and protects us from ourselves. For those not naturally gifted with a strong sense of self-awareness, a guy like Paul can steer them away from self-destructive behavior.

In Proverbs 27:17, we learn that "As iron sharpens iron, so one man sharpens another." It's a nice reminder that it's our duty as Christian men to help keep our brothers on track. Life's journey is filled with potholes, bumps, and blind curves. Having someone to help you navigate the highways and byways of life is a precious gift. Embrace the tough conversations.

MY PRAYER
God, surround me with men who will counsel and guide me on this journey. Soften my heart so that I can receive their words of rebuke, direction, and encouragement in the spirit in which they are intended. Give me the blessing of relationship so that I may speak truth to other men. I pray for these things in the name of your son, Jesus. Amen.

READ: PROVERBS 27:5-6, 17

QUESTION #1: How did you react the last time a trusted friend spoke truth into your life?

QUESTION #2: Who could best fulfill the role of a "Paul" in your life right now?

CONTEMPLATE

Create three columns on a sheet of paper. At the top of each each column, write the names of Paul, Timothy, and Barnabas. In each column, write the names of the men in your life who fulfill the roles of someone who mentors you, someone who would benefit from your guidance and someone who could most naturally encourage you in your journey. Describe your reaction to the completed list.

I have been crucified with Christ and I no longer live,
but Christ lives in me. The life I now live in the body,
I live by faith in the Son of God, who loved me and
gave himself for me.

Galatians 2:20 NIV

WEEK 2

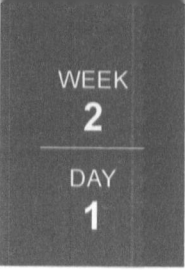
SAVED BY FAITH

"We who are Jews by birth and not sinful Gentiles know that a person is not justified by the works of the law, but by faith in Jesus Christ. So, we, too, have put our faith in Christ Jesus that we may be justified by faith in Christ and not by the works of the law, because by the works of the law no one will be justified." Galatians 2:15-16

A great source of consternation for Paul was the false teaching by Judaizers that those who wanted to be in good standing with God would also have to adhere to the tenets of Mosaic law found in the Torah. The central point of contention for Paul specifically dealt with the requirement that men be circumcised. Paul strongly objected to this teaching, noting that because Christ died on the cross for our sins, our faith in Christ was all that was needed to be justified in the eyes of God. Paul insisted that men should not place a greater emphasis on adhering to the law than on deepening their faith in Christ Jesus.

In Colossians 1:21-22, we are reminded that man first became alienated from God because of sin. We only became holy and unblemished in God's sight because of the physical and human death of Christ. As men grew more distant from God over the centuries, a prescribed set of laws were sent through Moses as a placeholder until Jesus could be sent to forgive us of the sin that separated us from God. Once Jesus came and died, Paul rightly professed that the importance and purpose of the law had been greatly diminished.

We could make an excellent case that following the Ten Commandments as revealed by Moses is a good and right thing to do. However, that was not Paul's point. Because of our sin, our only hope for salvation is made possible by the overwhelming sacrifice of Christ on the cross. Through that act, and that act alone, we became reconciled with God. Paul further argued that it was impossible for man to be in complete compliance with the law. While the laws could guide us, they could not save us.

The sacrifice of Christ does not give us a license to sin and abandon the laws that have been set forth. The law still serves the valuable purpose of guiding us, guarding us from sin, and establishing a set standard for behavior. We are still expected to live lives that demonstrate our love for God and his people. By God's mercy, we have been redeemed through Christ and it will be our faith, and only our faith, which will be the reason for our eternal life in God's heaven.

MY PRAYER
God, I thank you for the sacrifice of Jesus, which covered my sins and justified me in your sight. Your mercy and grace are an undeserved gift. Let me live a life that is worthy of these gifts by honoring you while I serve others. For these things I pray in the name of your son, Jesus. Amen.

READ: COLOSSIANS 1:21-23

QUESTION #1: Does the knowledge that your sins (past, present, and future) have been forgiven affect your daily behavior?

QUESTION #2: What changes could you make in your life to make you feel more worthy of the sacrifice made by Christ?

CONTEMPLATE

Write a letter to God thanking him for his gift of mercy.

AN EXCHANGED LIFE

I have been crucified with Christ and I no longer live, but Christ lives in me. The life I now live in the body, I live by faith in the Son of God, who loved me and gave himself for me. Galatians 2:20 NIV

Have you ever known someone who decided to make big changes in the way they were living their life? Perhaps this change was spurred by a major event or series of circumstances that made it clear that their previous way of living no longer works. Paul made a bold proclamation when he announced that all of us had been united with Christ by his death on the cross. Gone was the old self with its sinful nature. Our old way of living had been crucified with Christ. Our selfish desires and sinful nature could now come to an end. Our thoughts and deeds would no longer be centered on ourselves, but rather on Christ.

Paul wanted us to understand that Christ lives in each of us through the power of the Holy Spirit. If we could deny ourselves the things we once desired in this world, our lives would be transformed. What does it mean to deny yourself? For most of us, this would be a radical change in the way we approach most things in life. As men, we've been conditioned to pursue life with a gusto that gives us an edge over those who choose not to pursue all this worldly life offers. For the first time in our lives, we may determine that it's in our best interest to stop rowing upstream and exchange our worldly desires for a life with God.

For men, the concept of surrendering has always been characterized as an act of weakness. When we give up, we give control to something or someone other than ourselves. For most, surrendering equals failure, and no man likes to fail, regardless of what's at stake. What we fail to understand is that the act of surrendering can be a liberating moment in our lives that brings with it rewards and benefits beyond our wildest expectations.

Be aware that this exchange comes with a price. We cannot live with one foot firmly planted in our old lives while dipping our toes in the waters of our new life. If we give ourselves entirely to Christ, there will be no regrets and no looking back. When we give Christ permission to take up residence within us, we suddenly get the benefit of his guidance and empowerment. We are transformed from the inside out. His indwelling presence gives us superpowers we never imagined we would have.

MY PRAYER

God, give me the wisdom and courage to exchange my life for a life where Christ lives in me. Let the Holy Spirit guide my thoughts and actions in a manner that yields a transformed life filled with the love of Jesus. For these things I pray in the name of your son, Jesus. Amen

READ: ROMANS 12:1-2

QUESTION #1: How different would your life look if Christ were to live in you?

QUESTION #2: What's the downside associated with surrendering control of your life over to God?

CONTEMPLATE

Write a letter to God giving him permission to take up residence in your life.

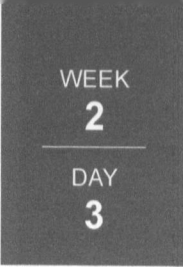

KEEPING THE FAITH

So also Abraham "believed God, and it was credited to him as righteousness."[a] Understand, then, that those who have faith are children of Abraham. Galatians 3:6-7 NIV

More than 400 years before Moses received the Ten Commandments on Mount Sinai, God had made a covenant with Abraham that included the promise of multiple generations, divine protection, and that his descendants would be a blessing to many people. The fact that Abraham was very old at the time and had no offspring may have made this covenant seem like a fairy tale or empty promise, but Abraham had great faith in God and in his word. Paul used the story of Abraham to prove his point that faithfulness was all that was needed to earn salvation. For that reason, Abraham and the promises made to him by God serve as a mainstay in both the Old and New Testaments. Moreover, the importance of one's faith over one's adherence to the law stands uncontested thousands of years later.

Have you ever lost faith in another person? Have you ever experienced a moment in your life when your faith was shaken? We all have. Humans tend to break promises and falter on important commitments. Trust has become an important currency in recent years because it's become such a rare commodity. It's one of reason why so many men have difficulty building a circle of trusted friends and confidants to help them navigate life. As a society, we've lost our faith in politicians, governments, and, sadly, church leaders. If we can't trust our leaders, how will we ever trust the common people we encounter through the course of our daily lives? Yes, we have all been disappointed, betrayed, and suffered loss, but it's how we navigate our lives and relationships with God during these times that causes us to grow.

Paul wanted the Galatians to know that they could place their complete trust in God because he keeps his promises. When we put our faith in God, we become members of a prestigious family. We become the children of Abraham. The human birth of Jesus was the absolute fulfillment of God's promise to Abraham. It was a promise made, delivered, and fulfilled. As followers of Christ, we do not have to put our trust in our fellow man. Putting our complete faith in Jesus and accepting his gift of salvation is all we need to thrive in God's kingdom. That was Paul's point more than 2,000 years ago, and that promise stands as firm today as it stood with Abraham.

MY PRAYER

God, give me just a small portion of the faith that Abraham had in you. When I become discouraged and disheartened with my circumstances, make me mindful of your promise to me. Help me to grow in my faith so that the worries and concerns of this world disappear. I pray for these things in the name of your son, Jesus. Amen.

READ: GENESIS 12:1-20

QUESTION #1: What are the factors that prevent you from growing in your faith?

QUESTION #2: What steps could you take to become more trusted by those in your circle of influence?

CONTEMPLATE

Write about an experience where you lost faith in a trusted friend. What would it take to restore this bond of trust?

PROMISE MADE. PROMISE KEPT.

What I mean is this: The law, introduced 430 years later, does not set aside the covenant previously established by God and thus do away with the promise. Galatians 3:17 NIV

I n Paul's endeavors to rebuke the false claims made by Judaizers, he dwells on the indisputable truths of God's covenant with Abraham. At the same time, he chides the Galatians for their foolishness. The concept of justification by faith and membership in God's family is such an integral component of Paul's teachings that he becomes incredulous that they somehow missed something so obvious. He makes the point that in the same way a legal agreement between humans can be ratified, God's word cannot be made null and void just because laws have been put in place. As we will see, Paul is just getting started.

Throughout scripture, we find a series of promises that God has made to man. In Matthew 6:31-33, God promises to provide whatever we need. That promise is repeated in John 15:9-17. In Romans 8:28-29, God promises to work for our good. In Hebrews 13:4-6, God promises to never leave us. In 1 John 5:11-15, God promises us the gift of eternal life. Post-resurrection Jesus, in Acts 1:4-8, specifically instructs the apostles not to depart from Jerusalem and to wait for the "Promise of the Father," which was the Holy Spirit, who would come, not only to live in them, but upon them to be witnesses. Through these promises we can see God's unconditional love for us. We should all find a deep and blessed assurance in hearing these words. We should also trust that he will deliver on these promises, just as he kept his promise to Abraham.

In this world, where so many things sound too good to be true, God's unilateral promise to his followers is as good as gold. That's a hard concept for most of us to grasp. Perhaps you're old enough to remember the adage that "a man's word is his bond." Unfortunately, for obvious reasons, those words no longer carry the weight they once did. We live in a world where nearly 50 percent of all marriages end in divorce. It's hard to imagine a vow or promise that is more important and sacred than the union of a man and woman in marriage. Nonetheless, we live in a disposable society where even the most important promises are rarely kept.

For these reasons and more, Paul begs us to appreciate the significance and integrity of God's promise to man through his timeless covenant with Abraham. God's word with us is a sign of his infinite love for us. This is a gift that should not be taken for granted.

MY PRAYER
God, thank you for the promises you have made to me. Let me find ways to honor those promises by living a life where my word is my bond. Give me the wisdom to recognize false teaching and those who want to minimize the significance of your covenant with me. I pray for these things in the name of your son, Jesus. Amen.

READ: 1 JOHN 5:11-15

QUESTION #1: How would your closest friends respond if they were asked whether you are a man of your word?

QUESTION #2: From the list of God's promises to man listed in today's devotional, which is the one that resonates with you most?

CONTEMPLATE

Write about the ways you can improve on the promises you make to others. Do you need to make good on a promise that has been broken?

A NEW FREEDOM

Before the coming of this faith, we were held in custody under the law,
locked up until the faith that was to come would be revealed. Galatians
3:23 NIV

Have you ever driven a golf cart that had a governor device installed on the motor? No matter how quickly you needed to get to the next tee box or green, the cart's maximum speed was already set. You pushed the pedal to the metal, yet you traveled at the same speed. In a like manner, Paul wanted his new Christians to understand that their freedom under the law had similar constraints and were akin to the shackles placed on a prisoner. Once Jesus came, he liberated them from the law and gave them an opportunity to live new lives guided by faith, not by rules.

Paul was no stranger to shackles. Through the course of his ministry, he was imprisoned or placed under house arrest several times. His imprisonment did little to slow his evangelism and discipleship. Paul wrote his letters to Ephesians, Colossians, Philippians, and Philemon while in prison. He had been held in Philippi, Caesarea, and Jerusalem, accused of causing public riots, defiling the temple, and for allegedly being a member of a Nazarene sect. The metaphorical speech used by Paul to compare living under the law to imprisonment was his heartfelt attempt to help the Galatians fully understand the significance of their new freedom. We see the theme of newfound freedom repeated many times in his messages to these followers.

In what areas of your life do you wear shackles? In many cases, it is because we simply do not feel worthy of the love and forgiveness that God has extended to us through the sacrifice of his son. In other situations, someone has told us that we are not worthy. For some, there's a reluctance to accept this freedom because we fear the unknown, regardless of how promising it may sound. For others, we've simply grown comfortable in our sinful lives, blind to the notion that what awaits us is infinitely better in every conceivable way. Unfortunately, our imprisonment and denial of better things is self-imposed. We have locked ourselves up and thrown away the keys.

The reality is that there's a promising future for all who are willing to exchange their old lives for the new freedom found in Christ Jesus. All we must do is believe, receive, and then become a new person created in Christ. It begins with having faith that Christ Jesus took away our sins with his death on the cross.

MY PRAYER

God, help me to shed the self-imposed shackles that are keeping me from realizing the full potential you have laid out for me. Help me to embrace the new freedom made possible by the sacrifice of Christ. I pray for these things in the name of your son, Jesus. Amen.

READ: PHILIPPIANS 3:8-11

QUESTION #1: What are the barriers preventing you from accepting the freedom Christ has provided for you?

QUESTION #2: Do you feel worthy of God's promise of salvation? How would embracing this new freedom change your spiritual walk?

CONTEMPLATE

Write about a time when someone offered you a fresh start or a second chance. How did you respond to that opportunity?

But when the set time had fully come, God sent his Son, born of a woman, born under the law, to redeem those under the law, that we might receive adoption to sonship.[a]

Galatians 4:4-5 NIV

WEEK 3

EQUAL STANDING

There is neither Jew nor Gentile, neither slave nor free, nor is there male and female, for you are all one in Christ Jesus. Galatians 3:28   NIV

Throughout the course of history, we've seen cultures rely on caste systems to preserve social harmony. Proponents of these societal structures claim that by discouraging competition, people are more likely to be satisfied with their current station in life. They claim that these types of parameters and boundaries prevent conflict and unrest. That's a hard concept for Americans to grasp because of their belief that everyone should have an equal opportunity to improve themselves and their quality of life. Every generation's hope is that the next generation will progress and do better than the last. While opportunities clearly exist, if you grew up in a large family or work for a large company, you also know that there are still informal pecking orders designed to keep people in their place. If you are part of a minority group or a population that has been marginalized, you understand this better than most.

Paul goes to great lengths to show that God's family is different. Paul explains that men, women, Jews, Gentiles, blacks, and whites are all part of one giant multiethnic family of faith who share equal standing in the eyes of God. There are no slaves or masters. There's no distinction between those who are rich and those who are poor. We are all descendants of Abraham and equal heirs to God's kingdom.

When we understand the way that God views us, it becomes increasingly difficult to reconcile the way we treat others. When we consider the devastating effects of racism, prejudice, and poverty that still exist in the world today, we must wonder how many people have read God's word or been exposed to the Paul's teachings. There are a lot of excuses for why the world does not live in harmony. We can only begin to imagine God's frustration with our current state of affairs. The lack of unity in our culture can be attributed to fear and ignorance. We have a deeply placed fear that someone is going to get ahead of us. We live in ignorance because we've made no attempt to understand the hearts of those who are different from us.

God has laid out the perfect framework for us to follow. We must try harder. We must begin with the knowledge that the things that could unite us are far greater than the differences that divide us. There's work to be done. Let it begin with all who are reading these words.

MY PRAYER

God, let us strive to create a world that emulates the family you have built. Give us the courage to set aside our differences and embrace the common ground that exists. Let these efforts begin with all who hear this prayer. I pray for these things in the name of your son, Jesus. Amen.

READ: ROMANS 12:16-18

QUESTION #1: In what aspect of your life is there a lack of equal standing for people who are also members of God's family?

QUESTION #2: What can you do to promote a sense of equality for marginalized populations in your community?

CONTEMPLATE

Write about what it feels like to be an accepted member of God's family with equal standing among all its members. Compare and contrast this experience to your earthly existence.

GOD'S TIMING

But when the set time had fully come, God sent his Son, born of a woman, born under the law, to redeem those under the law, that we might receive adoption to sonship. Galatians 4:4-5 NIV

If you have ever wondered about the omnipotence of God, his masterfully created plan and timing of sending Jesus should leave no doubt regarding his power, presence, or sovereignty. Just as he sent Joseph to Egypt right before a famine and how he delivered Esther, an unlikely queen, to save her people from genocide, God's plans are always perfect. The arrival of Jesus was preordained and masterfully orchestrated. The good news is that God's power is exalted in us when we are at our weakest. Though we may lack understanding, God responds at the perfect time. Despite working for generations to bless, discipline, and plead with the Israelites to seek his goodness, God could not get them to comply. Just as the law was beginning to show signs of total failure, Jesus was sent to save us from slavery under that law. God had prepared the world for this pivotal moment.

When we consider the fragile nature of the world at that time, sending Jesus was an intervention of epic proportions. The world needed Jesus, and God had a divine plan in mind. Because Jesus was fully human and born to a woman, we could witness his full humanity on display. God wanted to provide the world with an example of what a holy life looked like. Jesus was human, but he was without sin because he was incapable of sin. Of course, God also sent Jesus to take away our sins. By his death on the cross, he paid our ransom and put us in good standing with God. Most importantly, God revealed himself to us through Jesus. Because of his teachings while on this earth, humankind could begin to get a better understanding from Jesus about God's true nature and our new relationship with him. And God used Jesus to destroy and counter the works of Satan.

As men, we frequently question God's timing and purpose. We often wonder why God has not answered a prayer or delivered a miracle when we've needed it most. We question why God would allow the death of a child or a loved one. However, when we look at the past, we see the signs of God's perfect timing. His works are wondrous, momentous, auspicious, and masterfully designed. For these reasons, we should put our complete faith into the works and plans of our good and loving God who sent his son to redeem us when we needed it most.

MY PRAYER

God, help me to accept your perfect timing and plan for my life. Let me be mindful of your power, presence, and sovereignty when I do not understand an outcome. Give me the patience and peace to know that all will be well. I pray for these things in the name of your son, Jesus. Amen.

READ: MATTHEW 5:17-20

QUESTION #1: What have you noticed about God's timing in your life?

QUESTION #2: In what ways could your life begin to emulate the holy life modeled by Jesus.

CONTEMPLATE

Write about a time in your life when you questioned God's timing only to learn later that God had a perfect plan in mind.

RELATIONSHIP OVER RELIGION

But now that you know God—or rather are known by God—how is it that you are turning back to those weak and miserable forces? Do you wish to be enslaved by them all over again? Galatians 4:9 NIV

All of us know people who are cynical about religion. You know the type. If you mention something that is happening in your church or at your Bible study, they roll their eyes and make a snarky comment under their breath. They are also the first to call you out if you say or do something inconsistent with the good, clean, Christian life you are pursuing. In truth, these people likely have a bigger problem with the people who espouse religious beliefs than they do with religion itself. Humans are not always the best ambassadors for Christianity. For these reasons, Paul believed that Christianity was more about relationship than religion. Just as Jesus was critical of the Pharisees, Paul disapproved of those who took a more legalistic approach to righteousness with God.

When we fail to focus on the relationship that we have with God and other Christians, we lose sight of one of the most beautiful aspects of Christianity. Our relationship with God is a lopsided transaction. God freely gives us his grace and there's absolutely nothing we can give him in return. The best part is that God expects nothing. We live lives driven by quid pro quo, transactional relationships. If I buy your lunch today, you're expected to buy my lunch tomorrow. If I help you move your furniture this week, you had better be prepared to help me move my furniture someday. It's a rare occasion when somebody does something for you and expects nothing in return. God has a different approach to relationships, and Paul wanted the Galatians to take note.

Paul chastised his readers, accusing them of falling back into the paganistic worship of false gods such as Zeus and Hermes. He warned that if they were going to revert to following the law, they might as well subject themselves to becoming slaves, trying again to earn favor with false gods by obeying all the rules, no matter how ridiculous they might be.

In many ways, we are not that different from the Galatians. We tend to fall back into our old ways and do what is comfortable instead of what is right. Paul reminds us to return to reality and see God for who and what he is. We can begin by humbly accepting his enormous gift of grace.

MY PRAYER

God, help me to turn away from my old ways and to embrace the relationship you are offering me. Give me the heart to model your generosity to others and expect nothing in return from those whom I serve. I pray for these things in the name of your son, Jesus. Amen.

READ: EPHESIANS 2:1-10

QUESTION #1: Why do you think the gift of God's grace is such a difficult concept for us to comprehend?

QUESTION #2: Which of your relationships is more transactional than you would prefer? How might you change the dynamics of this relationship?

CONTEMPLATE

Write about a time when you were given a gift that you did not expect or deserve. What do you believe were the motives of the person who gave you this gift?

WHEN THE TRUTH HURTS

Have I now become your enemy by telling you the truth? Those people are zealous to win you over, but for no good. What they want is to alienate you from us, so that you may have zeal for them. It is fine to be zealous, provided the purpose is good, and to be so always, not just when I am with you. Galatians 4:16-18 NIV

Some say it's a man's nature to become defensive or angry when someone challenges his words or actions. Apparently, the Apostle Paul was no different. One thing is for certain—Paul was passionate in his belief that the Galatians should question the motives behind the Judaizers' false teaching. And he had no interest in being subtle or sugar-coating his disappointment with those questioning the motives behind his teaching. Paul did not care whether or not his words would leave a mark.

When others question our motives or behaviors, the egocentric nature of our psyche gets triggered. Our first response is to stand our ground. Once the heat of the moment dissipates, a thoughtful man will analyze the situation and mull over whether those challenging us have a valid point. It's always easier to accept a challenge from someone who cares for us. If we believe that their words of concern are meant to protect us, we are more likely to take their words to heart and rethink our position.

All of us need someone willing to speak truth into our lives. Unfortunately, we can build up walls around ourselves and we make it clear that we're not interested in anyone else's opinion—not even from those who clearly love us. Sometimes, the people who are most qualified to speak truth to us are the same people who avoid the conversation for fear of our reaction. When that happens, the blind spots in our lives remain unchecked. None of us are perfect. Seeing the world through another person's eyes can be both informative and liberating.

It's important for every man to surround himself with other men he can trust. Finding this trusted circle of friends can be a challenge, but you will never know the benefits of true brotherhood if you do not give it your best effort. This sacred bond of brothers can help make you the best version of yourself by speaking truth into your life and modeling lives that honor God. Letting down your guard can feel risky, but the result is always worth the risk. It's important to encourage feedback from those you trust and whom you believe have your best interest in mind.

MY PRAYER

God, help me to take down my defenses so that I can hear the truths I need to hear. Surround me with godly men who are willing to mentor me and shape me into the man I long to be. I pray for these things in the name of your son, Jesus. Amen.

READ: EPHESIANS 4:25-29

QUESTION #1: Are you willing to let another man speak truth into your life?

QUESTION #2: Recall your reaction the last time someone attempted to speak truth into your life. How did you respond?

CONTEMPLATE

Make a list of the men in your life that you would trust to speak candidly and honestly with you. At the same time, make a list of men who trust you enough to allow you to speak truth into their lives.

FREEDOM THROUGH CHRIST

It is for freedom that Christ has set us free. Stand firm, then, and do not let yourselves be burdened again by a yoke of slavery. Galatians 5:1 NIV

You will see the theme of "freedom" repeated often in Paul's letter to the Galatians. Paul could have said, "You have been set free by Jesus. Now go out and start living like it!" The idea that Christ, through his crucifixion, died for our sins and made us righteous in the eyes of God was, apparently, a difficult concept for the Galatians to comprehend. Because of this sacrifice, there was no longer a reason for the Galatians to continue trying to win God's favor through good deeds or a strict adherence to the law. Paul believed, however, that their insistence on following the law was an outward sign of their disbelief in what Jesus had done for them. Paul felt as if these Galatians were trying to take out an insurance policy for their salvation just in case his words were incorrect.

If we are deficient in loving ourselves properly, it will show up in our refusal to accept gifts, compliments, love from others, and help in areas where we are weak. We will self-sabotage our lives and accept a lower standard of living because we feel unworthy of good things happening to us. We allow shame to keep us walking in the fullness that God has for us. We turn down or don't even pursue higher levels of responsibility and compensation or even higher standards of living. Throughout life, we encounter situations that may seem too good to be true. Maybe we see an item for sale where the price of the product seems lower than the cost it must have taken to produce. Perhaps it's an offer with absolutely no strings attached. We've been conditioned to cast serious doubt on these circumstances and question the validity of the proposition. It's hard to imagine a better opportunity than gaining salvation paid for by another person's sacrifice. For more than 2,000 years, a more appealing and attractive offer has never been made to man.

Even though nothing is expected in return for this gift, there's a hope that we will live unselfishly and avoid the temptation of selfish pleasures. Paul advises us to guard this newfound freedom and not to take it for granted. He hopes we'll use this gift to love and serve others. Most importantly, Paul wants us to stand guard against those who would enslave us again for their own benefit. That's a small concession to make for a gift that delivers God's unconditional love and an eternal life with him in heaven.

So, the question that begs a response is this: "How will we use this freedom that has been given to us?" Some will choose to live a less self-centered life. Others will see an opportunity for a fresh start. Others will seize the opportunity to make major changes in their lives and will love and serve others, make disciples, and change the trajectory of their family tree for generations by becoming transformed men of God. The choice is up to us. Accept this freedom and start living like you're free!

MY PRAYER

God, open my eyes and my heart to the full potential of what this freedom offers me. Let me honor your sacrifice by responding in ways that seem outside my current realm of understanding. Let me begin that process today. I pray for these things in the name of your son, Jesus. Amen.

READ: 1 PETER 2:16

QUESTION #1: Why do you think the Galatians were hesitant to embrace their newfound freedom?

QUESTION #2: In what ways can you begin to live out this freedom in your life?

CONTEMPLATE

Write about an experience in your life where you were offered something that seemed too good to be true. How did you respond? What was the ultimate lesson from that experience?

Those who belong to Christ Jesus have crucified the flesh with its passions and desires. Since we live by the Spirit, let us keep in step with the Spirit.

Galatians 5:24-25 NIV

WEEK 4

AGAINST THE GRAIN

You were running a good race. Who cut in on you to keep you from obeying the truth? That kind of persuasion does not come from the one who calls you. "A little yeast works through the whole batch of dough." I am confident in the Lord that you will take no other view. The one who is throwing you into confusion, whoever that may be, will have to pay the penalty. Galatians 5:7-10 NIV

In John 15: 18-19, Jesus tells his followers, "If the world hates you, keep in mind that it hated me first. If you belonged to the world, it would love you as its own. As it is, you do not belong to the world, but I have chosen you out of the world. That is why the world hates you." In this passage, Jesus echos what Paul has been trying to communicate to the Galatians. Following the example of God instead of the example established by man is going to seem counter-cultural to many. Those who go against the flow will face resistance, criticism, and rejection. Paul encourages the Galatians to anticipate this pushback and be prepared to stand their ground.

Modern-day Christians face the same dilemma. We live in a world where the desire to do the right thing is sometimes a minority opinion. We think we're making progress, yet it may feel like we're rowing a boat upstream. Making good choices and living a godly life seem to get harder as time passes. Even when we surround ourselves with good people who share our Christian values, we can still be under attack.

Paul is frustrated by the obvious relapse of those in Galatia, who had previously been making tremendous progress in their Christian journeys. He is astonished that they would fall prey to the tricks and deceptive motivations of the Judaizers. His analogy of yeast working through the dough reminds followers that faith can lift them, as yeast causes bread to rise. Yet it is easy to let negativity ruin the recipe. It only takes one disgruntled person to ruin something that should have been for the greater benefit of everyone. Perhaps you've seen this same phenomenon in your workplace or church. One unhappy person with questionable motives can breed enough discontent within an organization to destroy its culture. Paul warns the Galatians of the fragile nature of their new dynamic and encourages them to be on guard for attempts to confuse them and destroy something that was once so good.

Paul encourages his readers not to take lightly any efforts to deceive and mislead new believers. Trials and setbacks serve as great reminders that anything good is worth fighting for. We must all be vigilant and persevere through these trials because our enemies will be relentless, especially when the stakes are so high.

MY PRAYER

God, help me to stay on guard against the deception and evil works of the enemy. Give me the strength to persevere and the confidence to be counter-cultural when it matters most. Let me stand firm even when the world hates me. I pray for these things in the name of your son, Jesus. Amen.

READ: JOHN 15:18-19

QUESTION #1: Recall a time when someone intentionally misled you. How did you feel once you discovered the truth?

QUESTION #2: In what areas of your Christian journey do you feel as if you're rowing upstream?

CONTEMPLATE

Write about the things you could do to better equip yourself when your views and values are in the minority opinion?

FREEDOM TO SIN. FREEDOM TO SERVE.

You, my brothers and sisters, were called to be free. But do not use your freedom to indulge the flesh; rather, serve one another humbly in love. For the entire law is fulfilled in keeping this one command: "Love your neighbor as yourself." If you bite and devour each other, watch out or you will be destroyed by each other. Galatians 5:13-15 NIV

The freedom we now have through Christ can be a double-edged sword for men who lack discipline and clarity about their purpose in life. We have the option of using this new freedom to sin, or we can use it to serve. When we sin, we once again fall subject to the bondage and enslavement of Satan. When we serve, we glorify God through the various acts of love and compassion that we extend to others. Paul reminds us that we can choose to be free if we are willing to change our focus to the loving service of our fellow man.

As men, we are prone to disobedience and drawn to sinful behavior. Indulging in the flesh can take many forms. We can lust for sexual pleasure, money, or power. All these things draw our hearts away from God. These self-centered desires demonstrate our aptitude toward taking instead of giving. When we spend so much of our time taking, we demonstrate that we're not interested in serving others.

It's easy to see when we've stopped loving others. We become critical and focus only on someone's shortcomings. Rather than praising, we condemn. Rather than building one another up, we tear each other down. When love is absent, we become cynical and begin to doubt the motivations of everyone around us, even those we love.

Sadly, we continuously fall short of the one command Jesus tells us is most important: to love your neighbor as yourself. The best way to reverse this curse is to begin by loving God with all your heart, mind, and soul. When you love God, you'll want to do things that please him. Of course, God wants us to love our neighbors in the same unconditional way that he loves us. The best way to love our neighbors is to serve them.

How can we serve our neighbors? You can start by praying for them, whether you know them or not. Next, you can try to get to know them by asking about their lives and then listening intently to what they share with you. Find ways to make a connection, offer praise, and encourage them. The investment you make in loving your neighbor comes with the promise of a generous dividend. In addition to honoring God, each of us can make our little corner of the world a better place.

MY PRAYER
God, let my focus be on serving rather than on sinning. Let my newfound freedom be an opportunity to love my neighbor, pouring myself into the needs of others. For these things I pray in the name of your son, Jesus. Amen.

READ: EPHESIANS 2:3-4

QUESTION #1: How can you do a better job of loving your neighbors?

QUESTION #2: In what ways could you serve to make a big difference where you live?

CONTEMPLATE

Write about an experience where you had an opportunity to serve someone you didn't know? How did that make you feel?

FRUITS OF THE SPIRIT

But the fruit of the Spirit is love, joy, peace, forbearance, kindness, goodness, faithfulness, gentleness, and self-control. Against such things there is no law. Galatians 5:22-23 NIV

A mong the many benefits of our relationship with Jesus Christ is that the Holy Spirit comes into our bodies and gives us a new type of energy that transforms our ordinary lives into something extraordinary. Like trees that produce fruit in an orchard, we are transformed in such a way that we, too, can bear the kind of fruit that will radically change our lives. One of the purposes of the Holy Spirit is to help us live lives that more closely emulate the character of Jesus and to live out God's intended purpose for our lives. Without the presence of the Holy Spirit, we can do nothing.

One of the fruits of the Holy Spirit is love, which should be one of our superpowers. Love is at the foundation of everything we do as followers of Christ, and it is the common thread that runs through our service to others. Our joy is what drives our pleasure, happiness, and enthusiasm in what we do. Our peace is the manifestation of our lives being in harmony with God. God's peace surpasses all understanding, and it can renew us, sustain us, and strengthen us. Our kindness is the outward sign of how we serve God. It's how and why we show love and concern for complete strangers. Kindness is putting the needs of others first. Our goodness is what allows us to encourage and build one another up. It is what drives us to go above and beyond in our care for others. Our faithfulness is what it means to be steadfast, loyal, and consistent in how we live our lives in our pursuit of God.

We demonstrate our gentleness when we set aside our pride and arrogance and focus our energies on being patient in the face of adversity. And, finally, the fruits of self-control and forbearance give us the ability to restrain our emotions and to react with calmness and coolness when things aren't going as we planned. These fruits would not be possible without the Holy Spirit through whom Christ has gifted these qualities. As Paul says, there are no laws against these fruits, so we are free to pursue these attributes, and develop and nurture them until they become fully mature in us. When we surrender the emotional, physical, and intellectual aspects of our lives to God and bear the fruits of the Holy Spirit, we begin to realize the total potential of our lives.

MY PRAYER

God, thank you for the Holy Spirit that lives within me and the fruits with which I have been gifted. Give me the stamina and determination to grow these fruits and to live to the fullest potential you have planned for my life. I pray for these things in the name of your son, Jesus. Amen.

READ: 1 CORINTHIANS 12

QUESTION #1: Which of the fruits of the Holy Sprit would you like to further develop in your life?

QUESTION #2: In what ways can you tap into the presence of the Holy Spirit on a more frequent basis?

CONTEMPLATE

Write about the fruits of the Holy Spirit and how you see each fruit transforming your daily life.

WALKING IN THE SPIRIT

Those who belong to Christ Jesus have crucified the flesh with its passions and desires. Since we live by the Spirit, let us keep in step with the Spirit. Galatians 5:24-25 NIV

Our passions and desires can be a huge distraction for us. There are so many unsavory things floating around the universe that can distract us and lure us into places we shouldn't be. Beyond the explosion of internet pornography, men are bombarded with sexually explicit images almost everywhere we look. The national standard for decency seems to sink lower with each generation. What would have been censored from television just 20 years ago is now flaunted for all to see during prime time. The only way to protect yourself from tempting images and seductive messages is to go live in a cave somewhere deep in the wilderness. What's a guy to do?

Paul reminds us that our sinful nature was crucified with Christ. We simply need to accept our new status in the spirit and rely on Christ to help us conquer the sin that tempts us. Paul encourages us to take what is rightfully ours and walk in the spirit ... like we own it. To do this effectively, we need to shed our lives of destructive and sinful behaviors such as criticism, envy, lust, deceit, idolatry, and selfish ambition. Sounds easy, eh? Not so much.

In Romans 8:5-6, we learn, "Those who live according to the flesh have their minds set on what the flesh desires; but those who live in accordance with the spirit have their minds set on what the spirit desires. The mind governed by the flesh is death, but the mind governed by the spirit is life and peace." To live in unity with Christ, we must first learn to live in the spirit. Whatever we focus on grows in importance to us, so focus on God. Magnify him, and he will become larger than anything or anyone who challenges our faith.

Keeping in step with the spirit requires us to adopt a new mindset regarding the power that sin has over us. In our present way of thinking, we believe that we're weak and unable to avoid the vices that seem to keep us deeply rooted in our pattern of sin. Our new status in the spirit is all about mind over matter. Jesus is giving us a "Get Out of Jail Free" card and giving us permission to pull our shoulders back, puff up our chests, and take on this new identity. It's worth a try. You'll find that success breeds success. When you see the doors that God will open for you in response to your new way of living, it will be hard to resist the momentum that comes from walking in the spirit.

MY PRAYER

God, teach me to live in the spirit. Free from my life of the passions and desires that are rooted in sin and evil. Give me the confidence I need to pull my shoulders back and walk like a new man in accordance with the spirit. I pray for these things in the name of your son, Jesus. Amen.

READ: ROMANS 8:1-11

QUESTION #1: How different would your life look if you were to start walking in the spirit?

QUESTION #2: What are some ways you can avoid being exposed to explicit messages and images?

CONTEMPLATE

Write a description of what "living in the spirit" would look like in your life.

RESTORE ONE ANOTHER

Brothers and sisters, if someone is caught in a sin, you who live by the Spirit should restore that person gently. But watch yourselves, or you also may be tempted. Carry each other's burdens, and in this way, you will fulfill the law of Christ. Galatians 6:1-2 NIV

We've all known someone who has experienced a mighty battle with sin. Perhaps they've experienced an addiction to alcohol, drugs, or pornography. Maybe they've struggled with fidelity in their marriage, trying unsuccessfully to resist the temptation of an extramarital affair. Whatever the sin, there are times when we feel as if we are being held hostage by it. Despite our best intentions, we often feel powerless in our efforts to fight back the forces that are pulling us toward this sin.

Unfortunately, our proclivity toward weakness can do great damage to our relationships as well as to our physical and mental health. In this passage, Paul calls on us to rescue one another from this sin and to begin a restoration process that will give us our freedom back.

Is there a sin that you need to be rescued from? Do you have an ally who can help walk you through the restoration process? As with so many addictions, recovery begins by simply acknowledging to others that this sin exists in your life. Even though you will feel hesitant to do so, you'll need to admit that you're trapped and that you feel unable to address this issue on your own. This step requires tremendous courage. There's no shame in this, and it's important for you to know that you are not alone. In Romans 3:23, we are reminded that "all have sinned and fallen short of the glory of God."

We've talked before about the importance of surrounding yourself with other godly men who can help you navigate life's detours. When a person is controlled by their own sin, they need a trusted friend to share the burden, assure them, and gently help them understand the power of this sin. There used to be a joke that said, "A real man never stops and asks for directions." Long before GPS, we relied on paper roadmaps to get us from one location to another. Today, all we need is a mobile device to tell us we've made a wrong turn with suggestions for how to get back on the right path. While technology and wayfinding have come a long way, men are still stubborn and unlikely to ask for help. You're going to have to dig deep, swallow your pride, and then ask for help.

Your freedom from this sin is nearer than you think. Surrender to the reality that you cannot do this on your own and ask a trusted friend to help you restore your life. You'll be so glad you did.

MY PRAYER

God, help me to recognize the sin that controls my life and give me the courage to ask for help. Give me a heart that is willing to do the same for the men in my life who are struggling with sin. Let us share one another's burdens and follow a path that leads to restoration. I pray for these things in the name of your son, Jesus. Amen.

READ: ROMANS 3:9-23

QUESTION #1: When you look objectively at your life, is there a sin that has the potential to grow and dominate you right now?

QUESTION #2: Why do you believe Paul warns his readers in Galatians 6:1 to, "watch yourselves, or you may be tempted"? What is Paul trying to tell us?

CONTEMPLATE

Make a list of the trusted friends in your network with whom you feel comfortable sharing your struggle with sin. Write about the factors that may be preventing you from taking the bold step of asking for their help.

Each one should test their own actions.
Then they can take pride in themselves alone,
without comparing themselves to someone else,
for each one should carry their own load.

Galatians 6:4-5 NIV

WEEK 5

COMPARISON

Each one should test their own actions. Then they can take pride in themselves alone, without comparing themselves to someone else, for each one should carry their own load. Galatians 6:4-5 NIV

One of my favorite quotes of all time comes from the 26th president of the United States, Theodore Roosevelt, who said, "Comparison is the thief of joy." It's likely that Roosevelt was inspired by this passage in Galatians, where Paul encourages his readers to count their own fortunes and be less worried about the actions of their neighbors. President Roosevelt was known for his exuberant and cheerful personality despite the many tragedies in his life. As a child, he suffered terribly with asthma. In 1884, both his wife and his mother died on the same night. At age 42, after the assassination of William McKinley, Roosevelt became the youngest president to serve our country. Despite all this tragedy, he could still find a reason for joy. Though historians have largely ignored this aspect of his life, Roosevelt was a devout Christian. He often leaned into his faith by quoting scripture in his speeches and in his writings on the Christian's role in modern society.

As men, we spend a lot of time measuring our personal circumstances and accomplishments and then stacking them up in comparison to others. We seem to obsess over who drives a nicer truck, lives in a nicer home, or who has a prettier girl on his arm. These obsessions are wildly amplified in this era of social media where there's an inclination by so many to post only the best and brightest aspects of their lives for the world to see. You don't have to spend a lot of time on social media to see someone's new hairstyle, their new car, the latest photographs of their beautiful family, or a photo of the perfect chocolate soufflé. We somehow fail to make the connection that our "friends" are only posting what they want us to see. We end up comparing our lowest valleys to someone else's highest mountains. We don't get to see the dirty dishes in their kitchen sink, the vomit stain on their dining room floor, or the inside of their closets. Too much time on social media can make us feel inadequate and inferior.

In Philippians 4:12, Paul shares that he has "learned the secret of being content no matter what happens." Rather than comparing our fortunes or misfortunes against those of others, Paul instructs us to adopt a mindset of gratitude. Rather than focusing on what we don't have, focus instead on the many blessings God has granted and made possible in our lives. Having an "attitude of gratitude" will shift our perspective about our lives.

MY PRAYER

God, make me mindful of the blessings in my life and turn my focus inward as I assess my current circumstances. Instill in me a depth of gratitude that reflects all that you have given me. I pray for these things in the name of your son, Jesus. Amen.

READ: PHILIPPIANS 4:11–12

QUESTION #1: How likely are you to compare the circumstances of your life with that of another person?

QUESTION #2: Would you be more likely to spend more or less time on social media if people were only allowed to post realistic and accurate portrayals of their lives?

CONTEMPLATE

Keep a "gratitude journal" for the next 10 days, recording the things in your life for which you are grateful. How many items will you have on your list? How will this exercise affect your outlook?

TAKING THE CURSE

Christ redeemed us from the curse of the law by becoming a curse for us, for it is written: "Cursed is everyone who is hung on a pole." He redeemed us in order that the blessing given to Abraham might come to the Gentiles through Christ Jesus, so that by faith we might receive the promise of the Spirit. Galatians 3:13-14 NIV

I f you served in the armed services, you probably have a better understanding of the concept of sacrifice than most people. This is especially true for those deployed during a conflict in another part of the world. Knowing that your life was in danger for the cause of freedom would prompt you to reflect on the deeper meaning of sacrifice. The gravity of giving your life for the benefit of others is reflected in John 15:13, "Greater love has no one than this: to lay down one's life for one of his friends."

Jesus gave his life for freedom, but not in a patriotic sort of way. Imagine, for a moment, the enormity of his sacrifice. Jesus gave himself to become sin for us in exchange for our freedom. God, who is omnipotent, chose to become a mere human. God, who had the riches of the world at his fingertips, chose to become impoverished. God, through his son, Jesus, who was indisputably pure, chose to have the sins of the world dumped on him. Imagine that the cost of every hateful, terrible, cruel, selfish thing that man had ever done was now resting on the shoulders of Jesus. The concept of sacrifice takes on a whole new meaning and depth when we contemplate the price that Jesus ultimately paid.

There's a tendency in modern society to throw around the term "sacrifice" in meaningless ways. If you're a parent, you may have to sacrifice sleeping late on Saturday mornings so your kids can play little league soccer. You may have to skip happy hour with your buddies to pick up your kids after school. Sometimes we must sacrifice a weekend at the lake to attend a wedding or funeral. The inconveniences we encounter as part of our busy lives don't measure up, by any degree, to the true definition of sacrifice. The way we talk and think of sacrifice is a reflection of our selfish hearts.

Jesus became the filter for the curse; all the curse stuck to him and allowed blessings and their benefits to flow through to us. He withstood a torturous death so that we would not be separated from God. Let us honor that sacrifice in the way we live our lives.

MY PRAYER

God, thank you for taking the curse upon yourself to set us free. Thank you for being an example for the world to follow when we contemplate the small burden of putting others before ourselves. Help me to pursue the greatest form of love there is to experience. I pray for these things in the name of your son, Jesus. Amen.

READ: JOHN 3:16-17

QUESTION #1: What's the biggest sacrifice you've had to make for the benefit of another person?

QUESTION #2: What's the biggest sacrifice that another person has had to make on your behalf?

CONTEMPLATE

Take a moment to write a reflection on the meaning of Christ's sacrifice on behalf of you and your family. What does this sacrifice mean to you? In what ways have you benefited from this sacrifice?

ABRAHAM VERSUS MOSES

Is the law, therefore, opposed to the promises of God? Absolutely not!
For if a law had been given that could impart life, then righteousness
would certainly have come by the law. But Scripture has locked up
everything under the control of sin, so that what was promised, being
given through faith in Jesus Christ, might be given to those who believe.
Galatians 3:21-22 NIV

U p until this point in Galatians, we've heard so much from Paul about the shortcomings of the law that one might begin to believe that following Mosaic law is somehow an evil or sinful practice. To the contrary—even from an early age, most of us have been taught that following and living our lives by the Ten Commandments was the best path to a righteous life. When you think about it, who could find fault in the good intentions associated with rules against murder, adultery, stealing, or bearing false witness against a neighbor? Similarly, not worshipping other gods or false idols seems like a reasonable expectation for good Christians.

As it turns out, one of Paul's principal concerns with Mosaic law was that it was impossible for any man, no matter how pure of heart he was, to be in total compliance with every aspect of the law. Because of that, the law can't give us eternal life because we can't escape our own sinfulness. Unlike the promise that comes from having faith in Jesus, the law cannot give life; it can only condemn it. Paul was making his best effort to convince his readers that the life, death, and resurrection of Christ had changed the rules of engagement for our relationship with God. The penalties for sin were erased by the very sacrifice of Christ. The law no longer had bearing on man's eternal fate.

In these verses, Paul argues that there is no conflict between the promises made to Abraham and those made to Moses. More than anything, Paul wishes to make it clear that because the law cannot give life, it has limitations. Because we cannot live up to God's standard regarding sin, we must be saved in an entirely different way. Sin has a powerful stranglehold on man. We were imprisoned by sin and held captive by the desires and passions that we knew were sinful and displeasing to God. Accepting the sacrifice made by Christ and acknowledging the significance of this act and what it means to us, breaks us free from the chains of sin. We are liberated. Our ransom has been paid.

MY PRAYER

God, thank you for the way you honored your covenants with both Abraham and Moses. Thank you for your willingness to redeem us despite our weaknesses and propensity to sin. Help us to become more deserving of the grace you have generously given us. I pray for these things in the name of your son, Jesus. Amen.

READ: ROMANS 7:7-25

QUESTION #1: What area of your life do you need to access then apply the empowering grace to make you strong instead of weak in your resistance to sin?

QUESTION #2: Why do you suppose man struggles so mightily with sin?

CONTEMPLATE

Review the Ten Commandments. Write about those commandments you believe are the most difficult to obey. Which are the easiest to obey?

ADOPTION LIKE NO OTHER

If you belong to Christ, then you are Abraham's seed, and heirs according to the promise...Galatians 3:29 NIV

All of us probably know someone who has been adopted. Even if you don't, you probably have seen a stage performance or a screen adaptation of the musical *Annie*. You know the storyline. Little orphan Annie endures the hardships and rejection of living in an orphanage for many years. The dream of all orphans is to one day be adopted by a family who will take them to a happy, loving home. *Spoiler alert:* Through a series of unlikely events, Annie is eventually adopted by a multimillionaire named Oliver Warbucks, and they live happily ever after.

When God invited us to join the ancestral lineage of Abraham through Jesus, we were adopted into a new family with riches by a completely different measure than that of Oliver Warbucks. All the promises that God made to Abraham were transferred to Jesus and then to us. Paul wants to make sure his readers understand that our acceptance into God's family and the rich inheritance we will receive is the greatest gift of all. Paul desperately pleads with the Galatians to understand the important distinction between what is offered in God's promise to Abraham through Jesus (and then to us) to what comes through their simple adherence to the law.

In this adoption, it does not matter if you are a Gentile or Jew, rich or poor, a master or slave; we all have equal value in the eyes of God. We have been given permission to confidently live as if we are free because we are indeed free.

God's unconditional and unbroken covenant with Abraham (Genesis 12:2-3) has been passed down through all of Abraham's descendants right through Jesus and now to us. With the anticipated return of Jesus (Acts 3:21), any aspect of the covenant that has not been ratified will be restored. When that day finally comes, Jesus will rule the world and bless it with a peace and prosperity unlike anything we could imagine. These promises are part of what is known as the New Covenant.

In Jeremiah 31:31-34, the prophet tells of the time when Christ returns. The Lord says he will "put my law within them, and I will write on their hearts. And I will be their God, and they shall be my people." Our adoption into God's family comes with promises that won't be broken and a reminder that we have everything we could ask for in Christ, and, conversely, absolutely nothing without him.

MY PRAYER

God, help me to celebrate my adoption into God's family and to eagerly await the return of Jesus. Let me honor your covenant with a life made worthy by loving and serving others. I pray for these things in the name of your son, Jesus. Amen.

READ: JEREMIAH 31:31-34

QUESTION #1: How does your adoption into God's family make you feel?

QUESTION #2: How can you use the story of this adoption to bring others closer to God?

CONTEMPLATE

Recall a time when a loved one or trusted friend broke an important promise to you. How did that make you feel? How is God's promise different?

DEMONSTRATING OUR FAITH

For in Christ Jesus, neither circumcision nor uncircumcision has any value. The only thing that counts is faith expressing itself through love.
Galatians 5:6 NIV

Have you ever known someone who abided by a series of game-day rituals every time their favorite sports team made it to the playoffs? Maybe they refused to shave their beards until their team was disqualified. Perhaps their "lucky socks" had to be worn inside-out during every game. If the winning streak continued, they were convinced that their rituals and practices were shaping the outcome of the season. Paul assigned about as much importance to the ceremonial practices of his fellow Jews as we might to our friend's antics on game day. He thought it was nonsense, especially since the coming of Christ had completely changed our relationship with God.

Paul wanted to make it clear that one's faith in Christ Jesus was all that really mattered in determining their relationship with God. And Paul knew that faith was best expressed through acts of love and compassion on behalf of others. The best way to check the depth of someone's faith was to consider how they loved others through service or how they allocated their resources.

There are many ways to demonstrate the love we have for one another. Beyond looking out for someone's general welfare, we have opportunities to step out of our own lives and go the extra mile for others. One of the easiest ways is to offer forgiveness to someone we believe has wronged us. As humans, it's our nature to hold grudges, keep score, and feel justified in doing so. Forgiving another person requires setting aside our hurt feelings or damaged pride, then seeking a restored relationship.

Another act of love involves building community among people who have disparate interests and agendas. Bringing people together to celebrate the things we have in common fosters relationships that can sustain us through challenging times. Eventually, we will discover that many more things unite us than divide us. Building connections can be tough work, but bringing folks together is where the payoff begins.

Finally, we need to be intentional in our acts of generosity. God loves a cheerful giver, and it doesn't matter if we're being generous with our time or with more tangible resources. In 2 Corinthians 9: 11, we learn that through our giving we "will be enriched in every way so that you can be generous on every occasion, and through us your generosity will result in thanksgiving to God." God gets the glory when we demonstrate our faith in the service of others. There's no better way to honor God than by guiding others to glorify him.

MY PRAYER
God, help me to build my faith through serving others. Let me be generous and attentive when in the presence of my brothers and sisters. Show me how to build community and foster authentic connections with people who are not like me. I pray for these things in the name of your son, Jesus. Amen.

READ: 2 CORINTHIANS 9:6–11

QUESTION #1: Beyond just giving money, what are some of the ways in which you can be generous with others?

QUESTION #2: In what ways can you build community in any of the different aspects of your life? Where are there disparate interests in your community that need to be brought together?

CONTEMPLATE

Write about your plans to demonstrate your Christian faith by serving others. What steps will you take to get started?

Let us not become weary in doing good, for at the proper time we will reap a harvest if we do not give up. Therefore, as we have opportunity, let us do good to all people, especially to those who belong to the family of believers.

Galatians 6:9-10 NIV

WEEK 6

HOLY SPIRIT VERSUS FREE SPIRIT

For the flesh desires what is contrary to the Spirit, and the Spirit what is contrary to the flesh. They are in conflict with each other, so that you are not to do whatever you want. Galatians 5:17 NIV

There's a constant tension that exists in our lives. No matter how godly a life you strive to lead, the battle between the flesh and the Holy Spirit is as ferocious as one could ever witness. Because these two spirits run contrary to each other, there is continual conflict between what we want to do in our self-centeredness and what the Holy Spirit guides us to do. In Ephesians 4:22-24, Paul tells us, "You were taught, with regard to your former way of life, to put off your old self, which is being corrupted by its deceitful desires; to be made new in the attitude of your minds; and to put on the new self, created to be like God, in true righteousness, and holiness."

For so many of us, it's a challenge to put off our old self. There's a rhythm in our old lives that feels comfortable and natural. Our instinct is to take the path of least resistance. Given the choice, most of us find it to be much less of a hassle to be punished than to be transformed. That's just our nature. The idea of "putting off your old self" is like taking off an old, tattered, stinky coat and putting on a brand new one. We exchange our old life for a new way of living, sin-free. In Romans 12:2, we are called to renew our minds so that we can see God's will for our lives.

You will find that the closer you get to God, the harder Satan works to distract you. When you're building community, being generous, or pursuing some degree of righteousness, you will feel the sting of spiritual warfare. Suddenly, you are under attack by the evil one and he is relentless in his efforts to trip you up. When you share the gospel and serve others, you may find yourself distracted and tempted by things you can usually ignore. Satan's power is real and, as men, we've got to be vigilant in protecting our hearts and minds from his evil plans.

It's during these times that you will find comfort by leaning into the Holy Spirit for protection, reassurance, and building resilience. The Spirit gives us guidance and the emotional resources we need to fight the battle and avoid the compulsions that can lead to destruction. In Ephesians 6, Paul tells us to put on the armor of God so we can stand our ground against the devil's schemes using truth, righteousness, and the gospel of peace to fight off the enemy. We should take each battle one at a time, knowing that the Holy Spirit has equipped us to win the war.

MY PRAYER

God, give me the discernment to know when I'm under attack by the evil one. Help me to overcome the temptations of my free Spirit and to embrace the promptings of the Holy Spirit in my life. Give me the resilience and vigilance I need to thwart the efforts of the evil one. For these things, I pray in the name of your son, Jesus. Amen.

READ: EPHESIANS 6:10–18

QUESTION #1: Have you ever felt like you were under attack by Satan? What were the circumstances?

QUESTION #2: What steps can you take to keep the evil one at bay as you draw nearer to God?

CONTEMPLATE

Write about the steps you can take to tap into the tools that the Holy Spirit has equipped you with to fight off the evil one. Do you feel prepared for the battle?

LITTLE SINS. BIG SINS.

The acts of the flesh are obvious: sexual immorality, impurity, and debauchery; idolatry and witchcraft; hatred, discord, jealousy, fits of rage, selfish ambition, dissensions, factions … Galatians 5:19-20 NIV

Perhaps you've heard the age-old idiom, "Give them an inch and they'll take a mile." This saying describes people who expect even more after benefiting from someone's good nature or generosity. Paul was concerned that some Galatians might be tempted to take advantage of their justification by faith and see no need to restrain themselves from sinful behavior. Christ has given all of us a unique opportunity, and some will choose to test the limits of God's mercy and grace. Instead of using our newfound freedom to serve, some will instead use it to sin.

Because so many of Paul's words had been twisted and misconstrued by his detractors, he must have felt the need to be specific about the types of sin that would violate our fellowship with God. Paul was particularly concerned with the sins of sexual immorality, impurity, shamelessness, and the lack of self-restraint.

Many of us believe, incorrectly, that some sins are worse than others. For that reason, we don't become overly concerned with what we call the "little sins." For example, when a married man stares lustfully at a woman who is not his wife, he may justify his behavior by saying, "It's okay to window shop as long as I don't buy anything." There are also men who rationalize their perversion of viewing pornography by claiming that it's a victimless sin. Sadly, recent studies show the devastating effects that viewing pornography has on marriages and other relationships because of its impact on a man's demeanor and temper.

In James 2:10, we are reminded that "For whoever keeps the whole law but fails in one point has become guilty of all of it." This is a stark reminder that embracing any type of sin can be a slippery slope for men. Our justification by faith is a gift to be honored and is by no means a "license to sin," as some would have you believe.

It's man's nature to do things his own way, however, this type of thinking runs contrary to the kind of relationship God wants to have with us. Putting aside our selfish ambition sets us free from the trappings that separate us from God.

MY PRAYER

God, help me to be mindful that sin is sin, regardless of my intentions. There are no small sins, nor are there victimless sins. Let me be vigilant in living a life that honors you, a life that is free from the stranglehold of sin. I pray for these things in the name of your son, Jesus. Amen.

READ: MARK 7:21-23

QUESTION #1: Do you believe that some sins are worse than other sins? What types of sin would you consider to be a "minor" sin?

QUESTION #2: Why do you believe Paul felt the need to focus on the specific type of sins mentioned in Galatians 5:19-20?

CONTEMPLATE

Write about the steps you can take to free your life from all types of sin. What can you do to eliminate the temptation to let sin into your life?

TAKING CARE OF OUR PASTORS

Nevertheless, the one who receives instruction in the word should share all good things with their instructor. Do not be deceived: God cannot be mocked. A man reaps what he sows. Galatians 6:6-7 NIV

Churches can be messy places. So many of us have such strongly held beliefs and opinions about church doctrine and the interpretation of God's word that we can be overly passionate about what would normally be minor issues. There are also those among us who hold houses of worship to such high standards that we sometimes forget why we go to church. Congregations are made up of two kinds of people: those who care too much and those who don't care at all. One of the toughest challenges of a pastor's job is managing these diverging interests and finding some sort of middle ground. It's not an easy job.

When you think about it, there's much more to a pastor's life than what you witness during that one-hour service on Sunday mornings. Shepherding a flock gives pastors exposure to the best and worst of humanity. Imagine being the trusted person to whom people confess their sorrows, sins, infidelities, addictions, insecurities, and moral weaknesses. Imagine spending a large part of your week counseling people through life's most tragic moments. Would you want to be the person being entrusted with secrets so dark that you become emotionally overwhelmed? In most cases, churchgoers don't expose their pastors to the joyful moments of their lives. Pastors tend to be the refuge we seek when life's challenges are too much for us to handle on our own.

For this reason, Paul calls on us to take the responsibility of caring for our spiritual leaders. In 1 Thessalonians 5:12-13, Paul tells us, "Now we ask you, brothers and sisters, to acknowledge those who work hard among you, who care for you in the Lord and who admonish you. Hold them in the highest regard in love because of their work. Live in peace with each other."

The next time you feel like complaining about the worship music being too loud or the sermon being too long, think twice about the impact your words are having on someone who has invested so much of their heart and soul into sharing God's word. What can you do to lift your pastor's burdens? What can you do to feed or nourish their soul? You can begin by taking a moment and ask your pastor how you can pray for them. Your investment in their well-being is a mighty investment in the overall health of your church.

MY PRAYER

God, let me be intentional in my efforts to encourage those who lead your church. Let me be the one who feeds the good shepherd with praise. Show me where I can lift the burden of those who serve in such a noble way. I pray for these things in the name of your son, Jesus. Amen.

READ: 1 THESSALONIANS 5:12-13

QUESTION #1: When was the last time you paid a compliment to the pastor of your church?

QUESTION #2: In what ways can you feed or nourish the soul of a pastor?

CONTEMPLATE

Write a note to your pastor offering praise and encouragement for the role they play in your life and your community.

REAP WHAT YOU SOW

Whoever sows to please their flesh, from the flesh will reap destruction; whoever sows to please the Spirit, from the Spirit will reap eternal life.
Galatians 6:8 NIV

Most of us learned at a young age that for every action, good or bad, there is a consequence. As children, we learned that there were reward systems in life. If we did something good in school, we might have been rewarded with a gold star or a spoken "Attaboy." Similarly, if we did something inappropriate, we might have been punished with a "time-out" or a lost recess. In the old days when corporal punishment was still allowed in schools, we might have received a swat from the principal or a smack across the knuckles from a ruler-wielding nun. These consequences helped shape our understanding of right and wrong.

Paul uses an agrarian analogy to remind us of the consequences we may face now that the stakes are higher. Most of us can understand the concept of a farmer sowing and reaping his crops. The seed that he sows in the spring is planted with the anticipation that the farmer will reap a harvest, the fruit of his labor, in autumn. Paul goes out of his way to make the point that whatever we sow, good or bad, will yield a corresponding harvest. If we sow love in the form of kindness, service, or compassion, we will reap spiritual blessings. On the other hand, if we sow sin in the form of disobedience, selfishness, and harm, we will reap the negative consequences associated with this sin. Paul tells us that disregarding the possible outcomes of our actions is essentially the equivalent of mocking God.

Sowing to the flesh is an act of self-indulgence where we engage in sinful behavior, pursuing our own desires without regard to the will of God. Sowing to the Spirit is when we selflessly pursue things that honor God. When we volunteer to serve others, show compassion, and put the needs of others before our own, we demonstrate our willingness to align our priorities with those of God. You cannot live a life of feeding the flesh and expect to reap the benefits of the Spirit.

A man's eyes and ears are the open gateways into his soul. What we see, read, hear, or imagine feeds our fertile minds. For that reason, we need to make every effort to protect our hearts and minds from the negative stimuli and poisonous seeds that surround us. Perhaps you've heard the term, "Garbage in. Garbage out." What we allow into our minds determines the type of harvest we will eventually reap. Let us focus our energies on exposing ourselves only to the things that will enrich our spiritual lives.

MY PRAYER
God, we are so grateful for the harvest and the opportunity to sow seeds that will produce fruit that honors you. Protect our hearts and minds from the evil that threatens to spoil the harvest. I pray for these things in the name of your son, Jesus. Amen.

READ: 2 CORINTHIANS 9:6-8

QUESTION #1: What is an example from your life of sowing to the flesh?

QUESTION #2: What is an example from your life of sowing to the Spirit?

CONTEMPLATE

Write about the steps you could take to eliminate the things in your life that are more about self-indulgence than selflessness. How can you shift your focus to loving and serving others?

REMAIN STEADFAST

Let us not become weary in doing good, for at the proper time we will reap a harvest if we do not give up. Therefore, as we have opportunity, let us do good to all people, especially to those who belong to the family of believers. Galatians 6:9-10 NIV

W e live in a microwave society. We've become spoiled by the conveniences of instant rice, soups, and puddings. Thanks to the evolution of technologies and online shopping, we're no longer accustomed to waiting for anything. As a result, we have become a society that demands instant gratification. We want it, and we want it now!

The same is true for our desire for feedback and results. We thrive on getting instant feedback and we are highly motivated by things that give us instant results. Paul reminds us that God's timing doesn't usually work that way. Whether you're waiting for a prayer to be answered or a sign that you're making the right decision, God doesn't respond on our timeline. He's got a good and perfect plan, and it won't come to fruition until he determines that it's the right time.

For most men, patience is not one of our strongest virtues. We grow impatient with loved ones when they don't follow instructions. We become angry with friends who do not return our calls on a timely basis. We become frustrated when others are driving at the speed limit in the passing lane of life. In Romans 8:25, Paul tells his readers, "But if we hope for what we do not yet have, we wait for it patiently." As he tells the Galatians, our efforts will be rewarded in due time.

If you're someone who has made a significant change in your lifestyle with the hope that your circumstances are going to improve, don't become disappointed when you don't see an immediate change in the outcomes. You may be frustrated that not enough people have noticed the "new you." You've done all the right things, but people still don't trust you as you believe they should. God's idea of the "proper time" may leave us feeling dejected and questioning whether our efforts are worth it. Trust God. In time, we will get a harvest of blessings.

In the meantime, we should continue to do the right thing, regardless of whether we get the feedback or results we're looking for. We should continue to treat one another with love, respect, and acts of service. When the time is right, we will reap what we have sown. When our hope runs low, turn to Romans 8:28 with the confidence of knowing "that in all things God works for the good of those who love him, who have been called according to his purpose."

MY PRAYER

God, give me the patience to know that your timing is always perfect. Let me find satisfaction in knowing that I will be rewarded for my selfless acts with the joy of knowing that I have honored you with my transformed life. I pray for these things in the name of your son, Jesus. Amen.

READ: PSALM 37:7-9

QUESTION #1: In what aspect of your life are you waiting for confirmation from God?

QUESTION #2: What can you do to foster a more patient posture or demeanor while trusting God?

CONTEMPLATE

Make a list of the things you've been praying for in your life. Pray for each of these things and ask God to bless you with a sense of patience for each request.

15 RULES OF ENGAGEMENT FOR SMALL-GROUP STUDIES

1. Nothing said in the group gets discussed outside the group!

2. Be transparent. Be authentic. Be your true self.

3. Everyone needs to share, both as a speaker and a listener.

4. Encourage one another. Speak truth into each others' lives avoiding the temptation to "fix" each other.

5. Challenge each other. It's reasonable to disagree, but respect boundaries.

6. Give your darkest issues the light of day. It's incredibly liberating!

7. Be willing to be vulnerable. Take a chance and let your risk be rewarded.

8. We all have blind spots. Dare to explore your own.

9. Absolutely NO gossip.

10. Embrace your mistakes. Take ownership of your weaknesses, knowing that we're all human.

11. Resist the urge to rescue others when they struggle to find the right words. Let people finish their thoughts.

12. Don't be afraid of silence. Pause and feel the weight of what has been shared.

13. Trust is our most important currency. Earn it and then be willing to extend trust to others.

14. Side conversations are a sign of disrespect; only one voice at a time.

15. When possible, find time to connect with each other outside the small group setting.

FredParry.Life

Becoming The Man God Intended You To Be

Want to offer feedback?
Write to Fred Parry,
711 West Broadway, Columbia, Missouri 65203
or email fparry61@gmail.com.

www.FredParry.Life

Other Books By Fred Parry

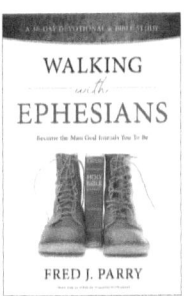
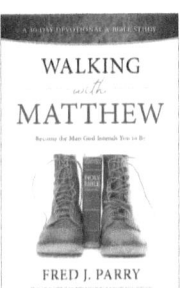

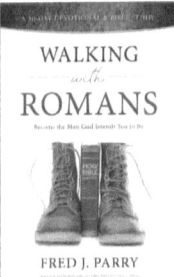

www.ingramcontent.com/pod-product-compliance
Lightning Source LLC
Chambersburg PA
CBHW030457130626
46549CB00007B/2761